AF209259

loud

channeled poetry & art

poems, illustrations and cover art

by mitra art

www.mitraart.com

thank you from the bottom of my heart

and the depths of my soul

you have allowed something that came through me

to reach you and be with you

thank you

not everything will resonate with you

and that's so okay

simply take that what does resonate

maybe it helps you to remember again

who you truly are

a creator

evolving and helping others to evolve

what we call **miracle** is more real than life itself

you are proof of that

Bibliografische Information der Deutschen Nationalbibliothek: Die Deutsche Nationalbibliothek verzeichnet diese Publikation in der Deutschen Nationalbibliografie; detaillierte bibliografische Daten sind im Internet über dnb.dnb.de abrufbar.

Verlag: BoD · Books on Demand GmbH, In de Tarpen 42, 22848 Norderstedt
Druck: Libri Plureos GmbH, Friedensallee 273, 22763 Hamburg

ISBN: 978-3-7597-7785-0

for my daughters

note

there are no page numbers

because

life is not linear

as you can see

everything

every page

already exist

all at once

simply go with the flow and trust

that you are exactly at the 'right page'

expanding and experiencing

what you came here to experience

you might encounter themes that are intense and emotional

be gentle with yourself and read at your own pace

<3

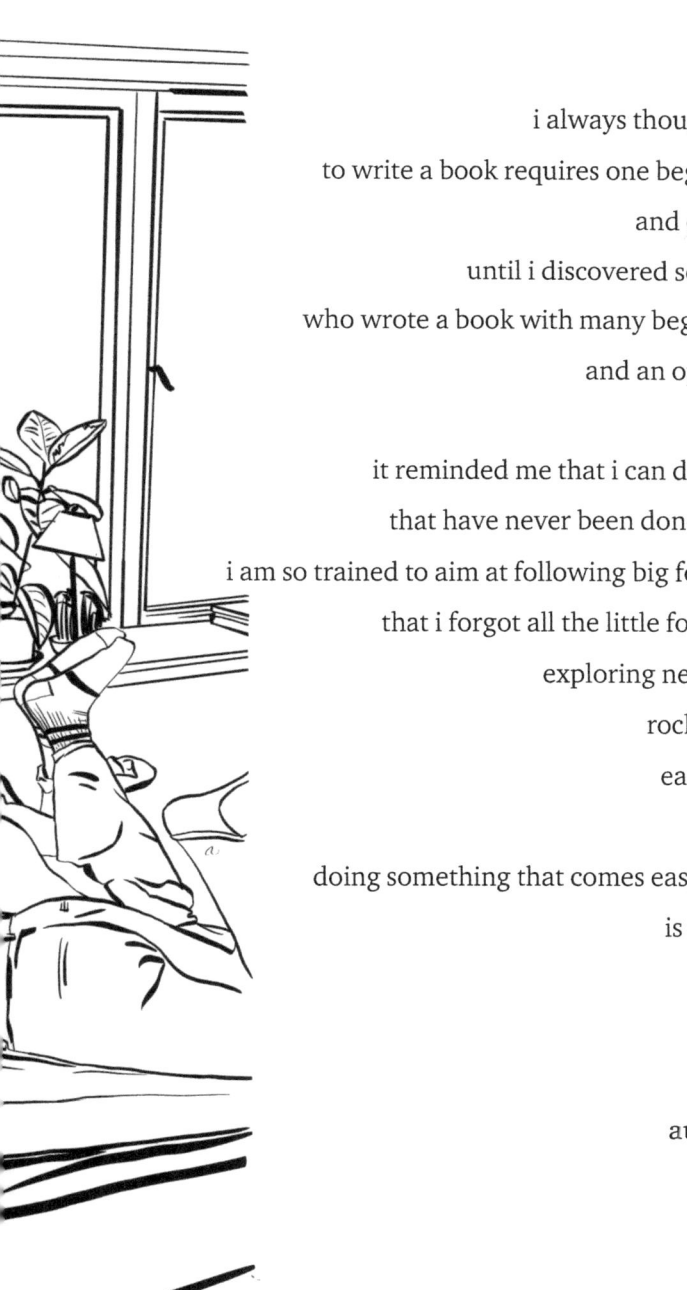

i always thought that
to write a book requires one beginning
and one end
until i discovered someone
who wrote a book with many beginnings
and an open end

it reminded me that i can do things
that have never been done before
i am so trained to aim at following big footsteps
that i forgot all the little footprints
exploring new paths
rocky paths
easy paths

doing something that comes easy to you
is of value
it's true
to you

authentic

i love green

green shades

layered leaves

when i look up

aiming to meet the sun

knowing that they will never kiss

never touch

but feel

but see

absorbing the sun's energy

and fueling a whole ecosystem with its power

only because they tried

aiming higher

trees and the sun

when meeting with nature

you meet creation

it's not human-made

it's energy

try not to focus

try to glance

than you feel calm

all is good

glance

my intuition is pure

my thinking is memory

combined it's a struggle

keep them apart

knowing which wisdom to choose from

when i reach for the sun

i grow

when wind is trying to blow me away

i grow stronger

when thieves are coming

stealing my juice, my powder

i grow fruits and multiply

when i'm drowning on a regular basis

time lets me absorb and take it all in to fuel myself

when i have done the work

i can show off my fruits to the world

then the sun rewards the survivors

the sun makes me sweet

red

nurturing

valuable and i multiply even more

tomato plant

you carry my weight

you are with me every day

you were with me in my mother's womb

you ran to rescue my life

you walked to show me the world

you danced to help me forget

you were still to let me feel

you bled to let me shine

you fell asleep

because i forgot you existed and needed rest

you were restless to keep me awake

you are a part of me

you do what i tell you to do

no words needed

thank you

for being

feet

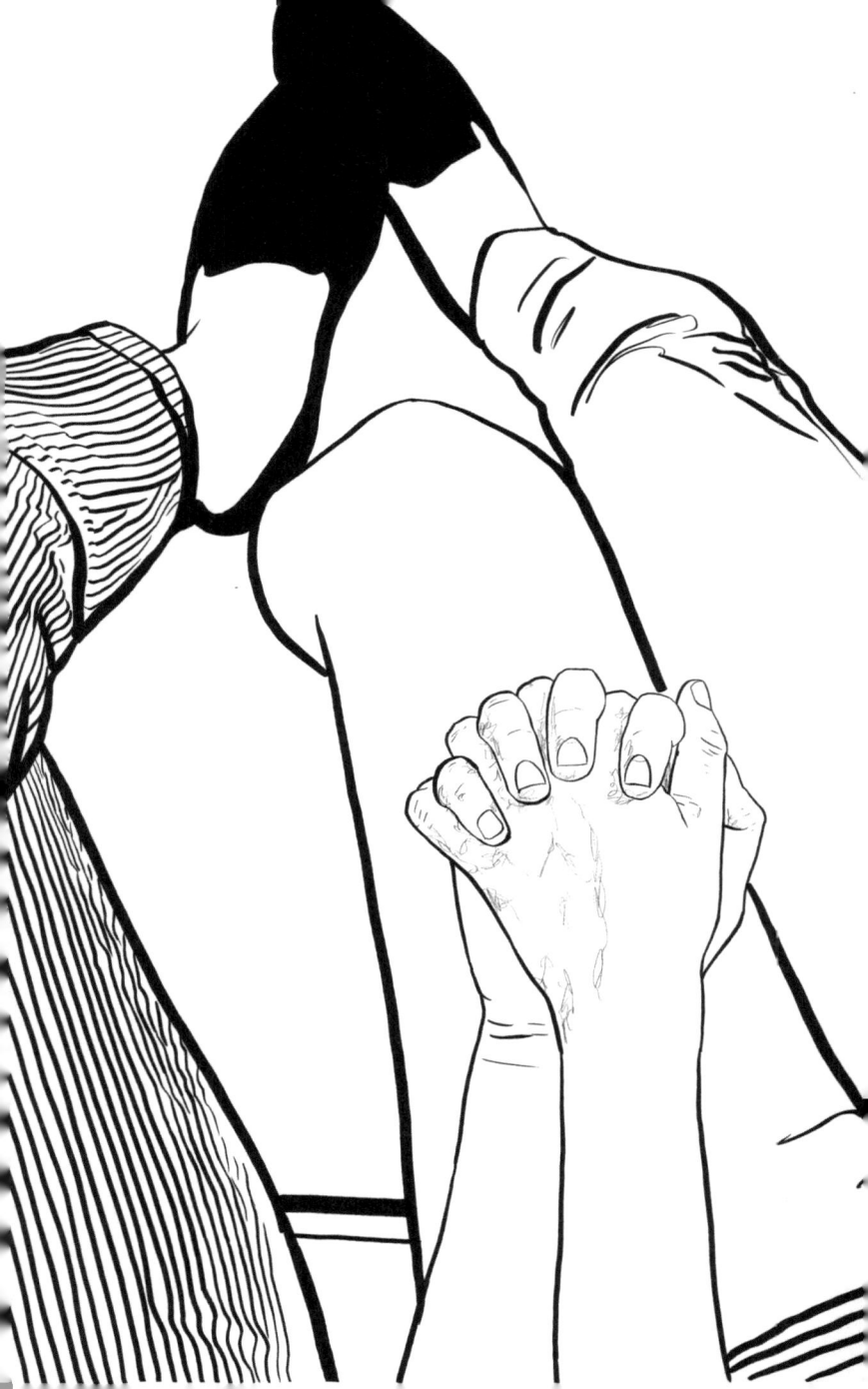

you require a lot of my time

because i need to hide you

because i need to get you

because i need to consume you

alone

because i need to destroy evidence that you exist

because i need to calm my nerves when you're not there

because i need to keep others busy to free myself to be

alone with you

when i'm with you

i feel ashamed

i need to stop seeing you

i am a liar

i consider the one person who knows about you

my closest friend

knowing about you and still loving me

you take up so much time

you make me sick

you make me look bad

feel bad

it's 'cause i'm creating a betrayal for myself with you

i'm masking uncomfortable feelings with you

addiction

you and i
are two separate things

i am a being
you are a being with me

i am connected
you are connected through me

i have courage
you are doing my courageous moves

i have intuition
you have memory

i have willpower
you have hands

i am the brain
you have a brain

when i get the call to leave

you are being buried and considered dead

because i am not you

body and soul

we are changing to new dimensions billions of times

while spinning around

when i reach rock bottom
i either have you or decide to give up

when i meet my fear
i either have you or decide to give up

when i start something new
i either have you or decide to give up

when i am the only love
i either have you or decide to give up

when i have no mother
i either have you or decide to give up

when i have no father
i either have you or decide to give up

when i have no brother
i either have you or decide to give up

when i have no village
i either have you or decide to give up

when i meet new people
i either have you or decide to give up

when i swim
i either have you or decide to give up

when i drown
i either have you or decide to give up

when i sleep
i either have you or decide to give up

when i pray
i either have you or decide to give up

when i open my eyes in the morning

trust

for such a long time i wasn't allowed to have one

suddenly i was suppose to have one

a very specific one

a nice one

friendly

sweet

but not too sweet

pure

childly

but not too feminine

not sexy

god forbid, my father said

believable

but please, please, please

not the center of attention

no

more like a friendly side note that everyone

will forget about

in school i was being bullied for you

you sound like a mouse, they said

can you even cry?

can you even shout?

can you even get angry?

they said while laughing

i don't know

i am not allowed to try

too much attention now

i am hurt

but my fear is stronger

i hope he won't get mad

i have no one

i don't have you

i'm not allowed

voice

freedom

we all seek you

but what you require is

what the least of us are willing to give

courage

in order to stand up when everyone else is sitting down

you need to have courage

in order to jump into water to learn how to swim

you need to have courage

in order to tell the truth

you need to have courage

in order to risk the known

you need to have courage

in order to run away

you need to have courage

in order to be able to say: no

you need to have courage

in order to be able to say: yes

you need to have courage

in order to be strong enough to take the blame

you need to have courage

in order to be willing to be wrong

you need to have courage

in order to be strong enough to listen to pain

you need to have courage

in order to be strong enough to say: i am sorry

you need to have courage

in order to fall in love
you need to have courage
in order to laugh out loud
you need to have courage

in order to tell your dreams
you need to have courage

without courage
you are living

with courage
you move the life of others

imagine

you have nothing to loose

what would you do?

you have nothing to fear

what would you do?

you have no addiction

what would you do?

you are thousands of women

what would you do?

you are light

what would you do?

you are being held

what would you do?

you are being heard

what would you do?

you have all the material things there is to wish for

what would you do?

you are being fed

what would you do?

you live in peace

what would you do?

you are healthy

strong

powerful

beautiful

what would you do?

do that

don't betray yourself

how to know you are living up to your true self

how can i fulfill my destiny?

how do i know when to say

yes

no

maybe later?

am i on the right path?

where should i put my energy in?

my attention?

my time?

my life?

me?

this question was haunting me

all my life

kept me uncertain

until i heard a voice

when you don't feel like you are betraying yourself

destiny

love

you are so overused

yet

you are missing

light

you are so accessible

yet

it's dark

god

you are in everyone

yet

we don't believe

intuition

you are the reason why we drank breastmilk

walked and reached out for what we wanted to explore

yet

we chose to listen to our head

wonder

you are behind our first wisdom

yet

we seek facts

water

you have memory

yet

we think energy is a myth

stars

you remind us how tiny our part actually is

that we play in this universe

yet

we think we are all there is

stop thinking

once upon a time we had seas full of fish

once upon a time we had the arctic full of bears

hunting these fish and fed their little bears

once upon a time we had forests full of birds

once upon a time we had trees next to trees

once upon a time we had oceans

and saw the sun rising at its horizon

dipping our feet to touch the waters

hearing the waves to calm our minds

listening to birds celebrating yet another day

once upon a time we've built a civilization that forgot

that cherished technology more than these songs

once upon a time we had houses bigger than our hearts

that blocked the view of nature we once had

once upon a time we were isolated

in stones, metal and glass

we called it our homes

we called it our pension

we called it our future

we called it our safety net

we called those who hadn't thought about that: lazy

and thought they forgot to think about their future

but instead the future was dead

they couldn't see

the view was blocked

their hearts were occupied

trying to break free from anxiety and social life

created by themselves

wild life

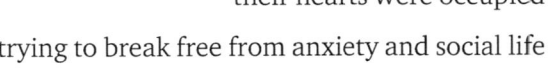

when birds could speak

what would they say to us?

when whales could talk

what would they tell us?

when penguins could cry

how many seas would they fill for us?

when trees could sing

would we listen to their blues?

when cows could live in freedom

how many drops of milk would they share with us?

when we would use our technology and wisdom

our companies and computer system

to free those

when we once chose not to listen

could we save what we've destroyed?

if it's not for those

maybe you'll listen to your future grandchild

who will once sit in your legacy

with masks, barely living

and feel ashamed of you

and feel abandoned by you

and feel angry at you

and feel hungry for the songs of the birds

the stories of the whales

the seas of the penguins

the blues of the trees

the rare look of the cows

living in wildlife

it's this thing we used to have

legacy

being r@ped

is a ~~motherfu~~cker

you ~~fucked~~ up my trust

my body

my self

my love

my home

my bed

my voice

my feelings

my heart

my memory

my social skills

my posture

my mind

my thoughts

my health

my sight

my connection to the world and all the humans in it

i am a ~~broken~~ human

rewrite your story!

tell yourself a different story
a story you prefs!
and act it out

you are the creator
create!
tell stories!
the first one should be
to yourself

♥

with a glorious soul

my soul is the one thing

you can't mess up

it's unreachable

to everyone

but me

rewrite your story

i fear you

you held me up against a wall

you pushed me back against my bed

you slapped me

you choked me

you touched me

you fed me

you ignored me

you were big

you were strong

i remember looking at you – long

i always thought i was fascinated by you

but i just forgot

i needed to watch out for you

once i saw similar ones

on someone else

a person i disliked

and realized

it was because of you

big and strong

hands

when fear comes up

when something hits you - triggers you

and you can feel it provokes a pain in you

it's an invitation to heal the thing inside of you

it's energy that wants to come out of you

to be released by you

you do not have to live with pain

and walk your path trying to consider

pushing that back inside of you

your baggage weighs nothing

when someone left you with heavy baggage

it's theirs to carry

allow the trigger to guide you on your healing journey

first - there is a thought

everything begins with you

every step, every written book, every building

everything we do as human beings

starts with a thought

the question is

how do we implement good thoughts?

to improve what we create

what we write

what we say

what we build

how we treat

how we teach

how we parent

how we dance

how we love

where we walk

how 'bout

when you open your eyes in the morning

say

good morning

habit

can you name twenty people

who inspire you?

yes?

then you are on the right track

you are doing good

because one to five are way too less

chances that you'll try to copy or idealize them

are way too high

also

i hope

nineteen of them are women

at least

because we need to celebrate their successes

and be thankful for opening the doors

for us to follow

read about their life and struggles

about their accomplishments

about their passion

and how they gained courage

fuel

i love myself

i love my hands

i love my heart

i love to hear my laughter

i love to taste my tears

i love my scars, my hair, my feet

i love my belly, my skin, my double chin

i love my weird teeth

when i look at the bite i just took

i need to smile

i love that i love to touch someone – just briefly

on their arm, on their back

to hold their hand one second too long

look in their eyes a second too strong

to show i care

i see you

i like you

i love that i can breathe

i love that i can see beauty in our ugly streets

a smile in a crowded space

i love that i can forget

i love my name

i love that i am a woman

i love that i'm strong enough to show i'm weak

i love that i'm brave enough to be vulnerable

i love the weird whole besides my ear

i love that i know what i know

i love that i want to learn more

i love that i'm an empath

i love that i'm energy

i love that i learned to love me

feels light and free

it welcomes more love into my life

a life i want to live

choice

how you look to someone else

is not in your hands

relieve

how you look to you

is in your hands

oh shit

where you are in life is 100% your own responsibility

let that sink

that's huge

it's no one else's responsibility

not your mothers

not your fathers

not your siblings

not societies

not the weathers

not even the financial crash from 1989

take it

there are two types of people

those who need distractions after their day

and those who don't

those who don't read books to learn more

about people who conquered a field

they watch documentaries to figure out

what's behind mystery

they listen to podcasts while driving

to master something they are longing to learn

they meet people

like minded souls

who uplift them, teach them, inspire them

they can't wait for the next day

to act again

to trust the way

they definitely don't watch tv shows all day

or meet up for coffee breaks to complain

to talk about someone else's pain

to get distracted from their awful life

distraction

i am a poet

i am an artist

i am a healer

a dancer

a lover

a friend

a smile

a hug

i am energy

like you

me

someone once pulled me out of my body

to save me

for what i would see

would feel

so i left

i came back

someone pulled me out of my body

so i don't need to forget

so i left

i came back

it continued like this for almost 27 years

until someone asked me

repeatedly

where are you?

did i forget to come back?

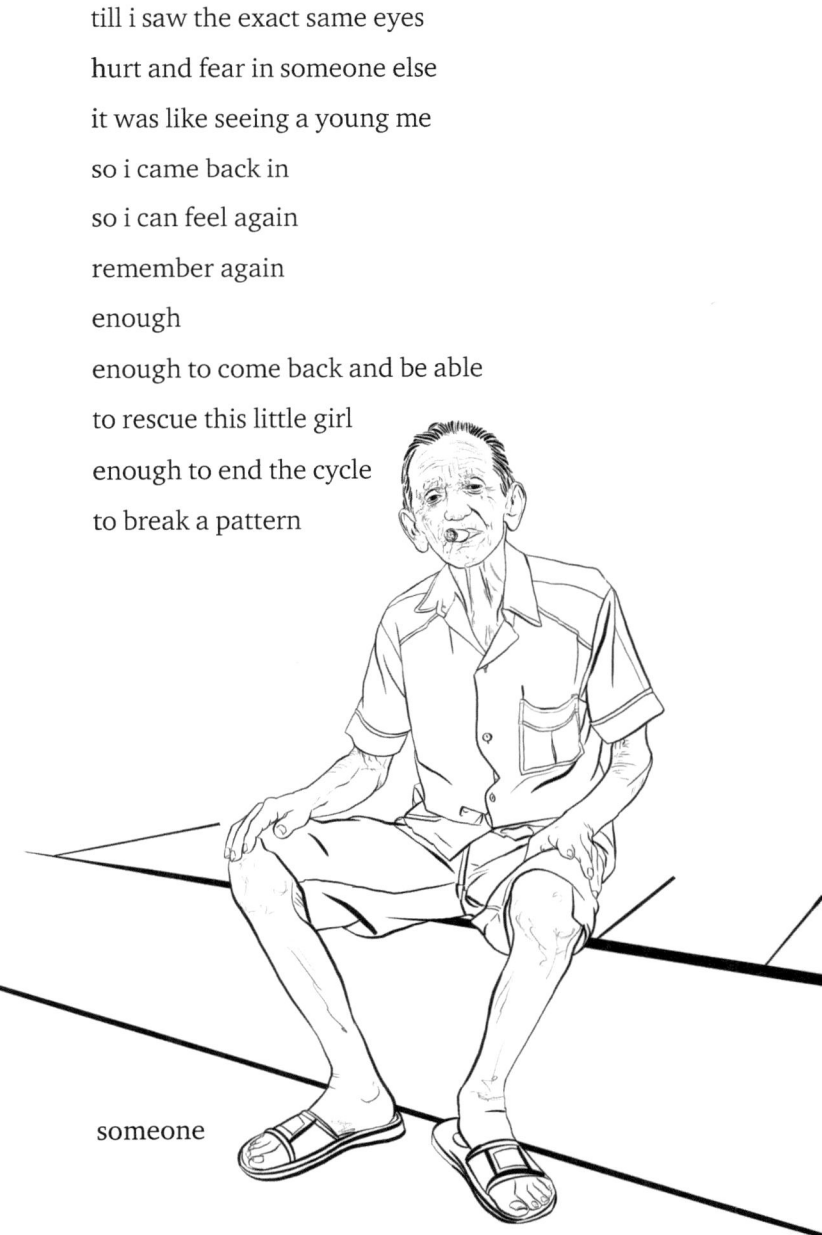

till i saw the exact same eyes

hurt and fear in someone else

it was like seeing a young me

so i came back in

so i can feel again

remember again

enough

enough to come back and be able

to rescue this little girl

enough to end the cycle

to break a pattern

someone

i love to clean

the smell of washed clothes

the feeling of lying in fresh sheets at night

the look of a few things i own in order

i love to see the immediate results

when you take a sponge and wipe

wipe off dust

wipe off the dirt of your past

the prints of your steps

to come home to a clean sleeve

a new white canvas to try again

when you cleared, canceled, deleted

what's not needed

beginnings occur

you= glass of water

every drop you put into you

consciously or telepathically

is what you consume

who you become

what you attract

because that's what you put inside of you

some aspects we can't hardly control in the beginning

like our family and parents at first

like our society and school system at last

but what you do can control is

who and what do you allow in your space

what do you listen to

whom do you listen to

what do you watch

how do you spend your time

whom do you follow

what are your patterns here

what do you consume daily here

watching on tv or see and listen to on your phones

it's called program for a reason

my coping mechanism were the doorway to my soul
i didn't know that
i only used what i had
when it seemed like
i had nothing

i only flew, because i couldn't walk or run away
i only believed in myself, because no one else did
i only talked to myself in my dreams
and visualized my goals
because in reality no one could bare the horror
of my speaking words
i only met god
because all the religious people told me
that there is no such thing as s... abuse in a family
and how could i dare talk about my own blood like that
i only created a save place in my heart
because i was scared to open my eyes and face the reality
i was born into

i only danced, so i could feel myself again

before i had to go back to numbness

i only listened to music to feel a higher vibration

because were i lived, there was no one alive

i only prayed

because i was in need to here that whisper again

my coping mechanism were a combination

of different healing strategies

somehow i must have known

someone must have told me

who whispered?

who saved me?

thank you team of light

you were always by my side

thank you

thank you

thank you

thank you

thank you

thank you

thank you

thank you

thank you

the only prayer you need

all the time i felt a need to hurry

i felt restless

i felt a hectic energy inside of me

i woke up with it for years

all the time i thought

it must be a painting

i need to paint the painting that releases me

that lived up to what was burning inside of me

now

while sitting here and typing like a maniac

over forty poems in two days

i'm realizing

it's the written words

it's writing this book that wanted to come out of me

it's these stories that needed my voice

restless

my urge to consume

what great minds said in interviews

feels like a preparation now

for what will come

when this is out

when this is out

i'm prepared

i will be the great mind

that will be consumed

but in truth

i think the great minds will confirm

it's not our minds that lend to greatness

it's the willingness to keep our minds behind

to make room for the greatness to come through

and shine

whether it's through me

you or them

the greatness is there

and doesn't care

through whom to appear

ego

i'm about to meet my altered

four days left

i'm feeling surprisingly calm

i haven't seen him for almost sixteen years

last time i saw him

he was holding my baby and then

we never saw each other again

i never heard from him

i didn't know where he was living or if he was alive

when i think

i don't know what to do

i'm allowed to be angry, sad and hurt

i'm allowed to say no and everyone will understand

i was the victim

i was scared for my life

he threatened to take it

he buried me alive

when i think

we ran away and brought back home by the police

they thought that's where we belong

we were choked, manipulated and spied on one another

to get some fake praise

we both were told that this is love

i saw him suffer pain

i saw him suffer shame

being massively bullied

then he drove away

the altered i once hoped

he would pick me up

he left me instead

to kill his pain with a knife that cut him deep

with drugs that put him to sleep

he suffered for so long

he suffered so bad

what a soul journey he must had

i believe he can smile now

i believe he can live now

i believe he believes now

in something called forgiveness

willing to be wrong

willing to need help

willing to let go

and stay

what more can i ask for

i'm willing to meet him

to praise him

to be proud of where he is and who he choose to become

i feel surprisingly calm

i'm about to meet my altered

four days left

forgiveness

we teach mathematics

we teach science and politics

we reach to earn degrees

we reach to gain profit

we reach to seek attention

we teach our children to become owners

owners of houses and businesses

owners of money and chicness

we turned art into gallery businesses

and homes into house investments

we turned music into productions

and mother earth into a planet

soon to be under construction

we forgot that

art, poetry, music, dance

meditation, prayer, stillness

are vibes that carry a world of geniuses

culture

reaching for the stars?

is impossible darling
it's scientifically proven

it's also scientifically proven
that reaching for something too high
makes you grow taller

like a tree

dream honey, dream

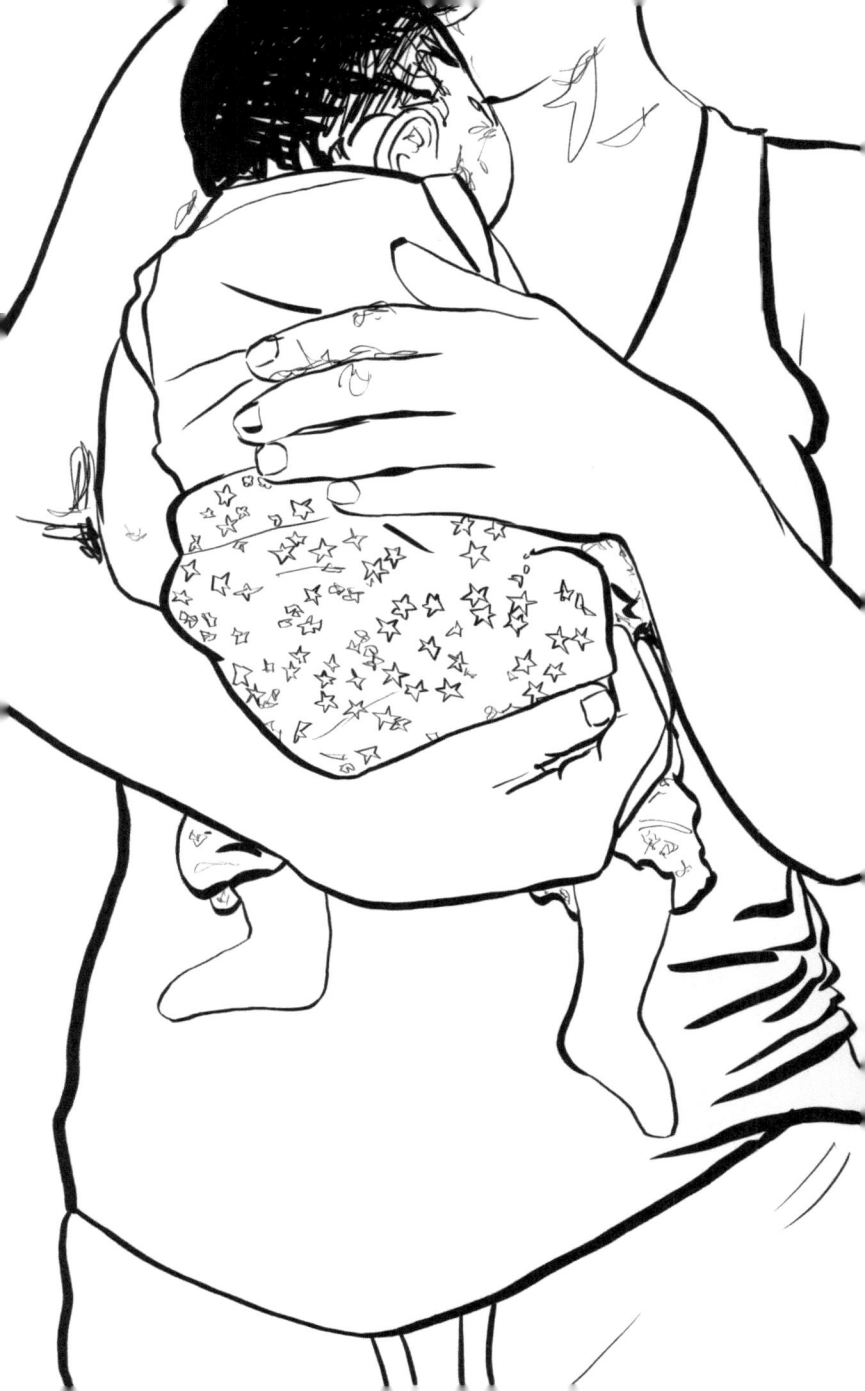

do you feel different from anyone else?
it's because you are unique
a unique aspect of creation
we are all different aspects of creation

you are not wrong
you are unique
we are all truth
that's duality

we need your authentic self
your special note, your unique frequency
don't shy away from standing out
from being the bright star in a sky full of constellations

by embracing your light
you draw others who shine with the same brilliance
and in that shared light

we find unity within duality

i'm pouring out my heart

pouring goes fast

it took days only

to pour out

what was there

for 39 years

inside of me

this book

a woman in power

doesn't take away the powerful seat

that is waiting for your courage to kick in

the opposite is true

she is setting the table for all of us to dine with her

rivalry is a false belief

i hope

specifically that all the mothers on earth

will release this false belief

and celebrate other women and their successes

teaching sisterhood is what we desperately need

no one wins if we keep each other small

you only reveal your own smallness by doing so

sisterhood

yelling is abuse

raising your voice in violence is abuse

controlling someone's behavior

outcomes and words is abuse

parenting through fear is abuse

using religion for personal gain is abuse

spying and allowing to spy on one another is abuse

removing love and affection is abuse

manipulating is abuse

threatening is abuse

making someone doubt their own perception is abuse

using silence to manipulate or control is abuse

dismissing feelings is abuse

withholding important information is abuse

conditional love is abuse

criticizing actions and choices to undermine confidence

creating dependency is abuse

creating isolation and remove connections is abuse

using fear, guilt, shame, doubt to control is abuse

it can be very subtle at first

be aware

just to be clear

what you can do to help a victim of abuse

is believe what they are saying is true

don't question their words

remember this

because what they have overcome is unspeakable

unwriteable

and all day long

for years

what they've heard is

no one will believe you

it's only bad for you

your reputation

your career

you'll destroy your future by telling

i will destroy you if you tell

imagine

telling anyways

after being brainwashed for years

after feeling ashamed for years

after feeling falsely responsible for years

and then you choose not to believe?

what you can do to help a victim of abuse

part two

be strong enough to listen

when they tell their story

be compassionate

don't break

allow them to break

offer your shoulder and wipe their tears

let them break if they need to

it will be a first

finding a soul that doesn't question

that believes

who can take the painful truth

and still be there to help

accompany you to seek professional help

it's the best thing you can do

it's the first love they will know

it's so easy

why so rare?

praying is a conversation
between you and creation
they say

don't forget to listen to her answers though
don't forget to be still and listen
when you are done talking
it's rude
i say

be still

creator answers all of your prayers

all of them

maybe right away

most of the time not

'cause the connection is bad

she answers through your body

sometimes

she answers through your intuition

maybe

through your dreams

maybe

through people you'll meet

or people you don't

maybe through doors that will open

maybe through doors that are closed

to direct you

to gently suggest

to look somewhere else

for the things you are praying for

your job is to work on the connection
to hear clearer what's been said all the time

also
learn to consider that the things you are longing for
could be the things least beneficial for you and your path

so trust
you are getting all the answers
and trust
that she knows best

connection

i failed so much in life

that i'm not scared anymore

i trust

i believe

i have faith

sometimes i thought

maybe it's not for me

maybe i'm not good enough

maybe i need plan c

but now i know

it was plan a all the way

all this time

the plan was to make me

fearless

oh lord!

that's what you've made me

that's why you put me through

all

of

this

to become

fearless!

world watch out

what will come out of this!

plan a

i am crying

when i read through my own written words

it's true

i have written them down

but never once have i thought about

what will come out of my mouth

out of my hands

my pen

i just showed up

and hoped to be used by the light

once brightened up my night

weeping while experiencing magic

i am so happy

i need to move

walk, run, dance, shout, sing and cry

i am crying so loud

so full of joy and bliss

why is it that we need to move and express

when in happiness?

but live in a big fat cloud unable to move and express

when depression kicks in?

move

crises

victory

crises

victory

crises

victory

crises

victory

crises

victory

crises

victory

crises

victory

crises

victory

crises

victory

life

rise up to your calling

you are a one woman army

arise

there are three things we feed our body

air

water

food

the third better be what the dirt grew

and offered to you

the second needs to be loved

it's energy and remembers the dirt

for the first one it's best to be freshly released

from the trees

now you have nourished all your parts that are seen

the home of your thoughts

now

what do you feed your soul?

it better be

the arts

soul food

i'm trying to follow my intuition

always

makes life easier

and worth living

genius

i once saw the story
of a rich white man
who went to live
to a poor neighborhood
as an experiment

he should live there for just a few days
he would have to sleep in their houses
and cook in their kitchens

but the first meal he wanted to prepare
was a rich white man's
it required some oil or fats in order to cook it

he went to ask the neighbors

can i borrow some oil?

he felt ashamed to ask for something so little

that he didn't have

his neighbor said

we don't own oil

that's too expensive

we cook with water

why don't you know that?

trash tv

how we judge people

shows who we are

how we treat friends

when they make mistakes

shows how we treat ourselves

when we make mistakes

observe yourself

being bitter
is like a disease
it eats you up
silently

being bitter serves neither you
nor yourself
it makes everyone around you mad as well

it's like weed
it has roots so deep
it shows your sad
you are hurt
very deep

you need to pull out its roots
but you choose to live with it instead
till everyone around you
treats you like you're dead

this only serves your bitterness even more
you think you have proof now
but what you really have
is unhappiness

don't be scared to pull out its roots
you're afraid it could leave a hole?
you're afraid you could pull out some dirt?

healing is what it is
a hole is only room to grow

avoid bitterness

when you open your eyes in the morning
feel what you feel like
how you slept
how it feels to stand up

when you brush your body towards your heart
to awake your system for the day
feel what that feels like
on your body, on your arms
and how the blood cells move in your veins

when you take a shower
feel what that feels like
feel the water running over your head
over your shoulders and down through your legs
smell the soap, and play with the foam

when you drink your first cup of water
which stood there over night
feel what that feels like
when it runs through your system
can you feel yourself awakening
your lungs, your liver, your spine?

when you prepare your food
feel what that feels like

always
whatever you do
feel what that feels like
hear what it sounds like
taste the sweetness, bitterness or sourness
see how it looks from the right, from the left
use your senses

it's called awareness

all of this awareness is preparation
it forms the basis for feeling sensations

one day, the nightingale of myth will sit in front of your bed

early in the morning, at a time when you're usually still asleep

she sat there many times before

but this time, with your awareness, suddenly

you'll be wide awake

wondering what sound touched your ear

wondering how something so familiar to your soul

can be so unique

training awareness

the root of all misery and fear

comes from thinking, memory, belief systems

and definitions that say all of this is negative

it's not bad

just be aware that that's not all

if you've had enough

decide to choose love

if you want to change your memories

your story

then forgive

jump into different perspectives

understand

allow yourself protection and distance if you need

forgive yourself for believing it was your fault and

let go

treat yourself with peace

a woman was once a girl

a girl was once a child

a child was once a baby

a baby was once a soul

who choose a journey to heal the world

a woman

my name is mitra

there were times

i wished i had a different name

more feminine

more mundane

it's the result of this culture

we have built

in which we teach

all the weird ones

should be the same

our children believe

after carefully watching how we treat

it's better when i'll be the same

otherwise i could be treated mean

or be ignored for good

let's celebrate our weird ones

'cause in truth

there is no such thing

we are all unique

when i have you

what do you do for me

that i can't do without you – yet?

maybe taking a rest?

maybe saying no?

maybe reading the book?

maybe quit work?

maybe make me aware?

maybe getting some love?

maybe getting attention?

maybe telling the truth?

maybe being more aligned?

by the time i answered that question

you lost your job

purpose of disease

finding the true me

imagine you have unlimited access

to the most powerful source of all the knowledge

in the universe

imagine you have unlimited access

to all the answers

imagine you have unlimited access

to energy that made you and me

now

close this book

close your eyes

breathe

deep

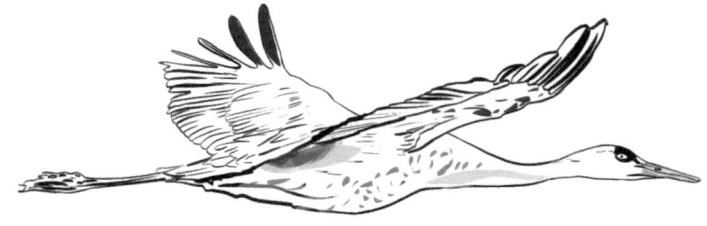

and use the access given to you

seed

soil

water

air

sun

a flower is born

stone

soil

water

air

sun

weed will appear

plant a seed

every year

i went to the big book fair

i had a babysitter

dressed chic

with my cookbook and illustrations

in my shiny leather bag

i thought

i will win, win, win

an eye or an ear

who recognizes what i can bring

every year

no one did

when i came home

i tucked my little girl into bed

and read her favorite fairytales

encouraging stories for girls

it was called

a little pink

a little red

she was happy

i was so sad

i cried in the dark

alone

when no one could see

the weakness of my bones

not even me

i couldn't let myself down

when i'm the only one around

they were not

ready yet

i had a vision
it happened twice
like watching a movie
except this one was real

i wasn't dreaming
and i could feel what the divine showed me
it brought tears to my eye
it was bigger than any dream of mine
bigger than anything i thought about

it was a feast
a celebration of the house i had built
standing behind me
i cut the red strings to welcome the opening

i was surrounded by family and friends
the crowd was full of people
politicians, children and some celebrities

i held a speech

a thank you speech

it was beautiful to see

what i had built was

a safe house for teens

a house of arts

of music and meditation

where kids could spent their time

and discover the magic and the divine

creativity in a temple

it was so chic

worthy to praise our true

artistic abilities

soon this will be spread out

through different countries

to welcome our youth

with the best of our abilities

vision number one

my second vision
felt the same
like living in a dream
already happening

i was walking along some steps
in a beautiful native gown
next to me was a big lane
full of people waiting in line

to get to an exhibition
to see my artwork
i realized just then

i hugged some of them and smiled
then i went to see for myself
i was so curious
if the vision lets me see
how my work is going to be
so i took all the stairs upfront

i was the first to enter

walked through the first majestic room

behind me i could here

people waiting to appear

i saw all of my paintings

room by room

with installations

all of them

i saw them so clear

the last room felt different

it was huge and dark

in it was a beautiful arch and a huge telescope

which you would use to watch the stars

when i saw for myself

it was to watch all of the other rooms

in retro perspective

what will you take from it

home and into your heart

that's the wisdom behind all art

vision number two

being aware

simply means

being present

without judgement

awareness

when we throw our trash into our gardens

into our seas and onto our lands

it comes out on the other side of our precious world

because we are one

because we are connected

through our sand and dirt

through our winds and clouds

through our rain and movements

when we are told to treat each soul

as we want to be treated ourselves, why?

because we are one

because we are connected

through the sun

through our smiles and tears

through our music and poetry

through our light and energy

can't you see?

separation is a myth

some people are bitter

they believe the world spreads out evil

only to harm them

some people feel blessed

they believe the world spreads out money

only to support them

some people feel poor
they believe the world spreads out struggles
only to weaken them

some people feel superior
they believe the world revealed different names for god
only to shine through them

some people are scared
they believe the world spreads out fear
only to protect them

some people are seekers
they believe the world is a classroom full of people
with different beliefs

be a seeker

when your child enters the room

look into her eyes with a smile

welcome her

be a friend

when your child enters the room

don't focus on her hair, her shoes, her dress

or how she walks

don't scan for mistakes

every child will feel the difference in this experience

being seen

when it happens
it feels like an angel flying through my veins

goosebumps

i didn't have a home
growing up

i didn't have love
growing up

i didn't have parents
growing up

i didn't have friends
growing up

i didn't have a voice
growing up

didn't have support
growing up

i had a roof

i had music

i had me, my higher mind, my soul

i had a team of light

i had dreams

i had prayers

i had faith

i had trust

growing up

i learned that

if you want to built a relationship with your child

the kind where you feel connected and loved

spend quality time at eye level

sit down and be

don't teach

don't preach

show up

maybe observe

maybe offer to do what she is doing - play

when you do that every day

for a bit

she will remember what you did

simply being there and offering your time and attention

will lead to great conversations and connection

when your child has a heavy heart

she will tell you then

when your child is unsure about something

she will ask you then

when your child needs your advice

she will reveal it to you then

when your child needs someone to laugh with

she will laugh right then

she won't do that at the dinner table

when you ask her how her day was

she won't tell you in the car just because it's convenient

build a connection first

early on

to plant the seed of love and trust

you'll need to show up early on

connection

have you ever entered a room

and the people were kind and polite

but you felt small anyway?

as if you did something wrong

that's judgement

that's energy

have you ever entered a room

and the people were kind and polite

and you felt understood and heard

as if you were seen

that's love

that's energy

thought is energy

when i was a little girl

maybe i was seven

i looked in the mirror

fascinated

how can i be

out of my body

and still tell my hands

to touch my face

and still feel the palms of my hands

slighting through my cheeks

like a miracle

i thought

that this could be

when i was a young woman

maybe i was seventeen

i looked at society

fascinated

how can i be

so sad and lonely

and still make believe

that i am functioning

i could attend school and go to work afterwards

having small talks and sharing laughter

while suffering the unspeakable

simultaneously

like a nightmare

i thought

that this could be

when i was a woman

maybe i was twenty seven

i looked at my symptoms

fascinated

how can i be

so sick and exhausted

and still continuing with my life as it is

i need to stop being productive

i need to stop make believe

it only serves people i don't need to be with

i raised my kid with all my love

and worked to grab out the dirt with a therapist

i choose the only two things i needed to do

in order to be in peace with me

start healing

feeding our soul is called

being unproductive

in our world

isn't it funny that something so essential

isn't even on our to-do list

hahaha

imagine we learnt to love ourselves exactly as we are

instead of training to be polite

imagine we learnt how to pray

instead of writing wishlists for upcoming holidays

imagine we learnt about meditation in schools

about energy and healing strategies

imagine we would be trained to use our thoughts

as if they were things and had power to change all things

imagine we would know all that before turning ten

how to be a healthy human being

dream school system

there is only one race

and that is the human race

i heard a wise woman once said

race what a stupid idea

how come we make stuff up

to feel superior

when in truth

we only function best

when in a healthy relationship

how small must someone feel

to be scared of someone just the same

just like them

how weak must someone feel

to be so cruel

and use someone else's suffering

race

when you appear

suddenly i can see clear

where i am

how i am

who i am

whom i'm with

light

you are not in nature
you are a part of nature

you do not have a soul
you are a soul

you are not your shadow
you are a light

life is not happening to you
life is a reflection of the energy you hold on to

facts

it's like attending a reunion

create a ritual to prepare your mind and body

for this event

sleep

look through the internet

the evidence is there

we only regret when we didn't even try

look through the books and magazines

the evidence is there

we only feel stuck when we hold on to blame

start doing

never too late for correction

never too late to say

please forgive me

never too late to peel off my mask of shame

never too late to open my eyes to see more light

never assume you are forgiven

never assume you are understood

never assume it could be easy

but doing it anyway

doing your part to change

doing what's in your hands

that's the only way

it's never too late

you can change you

growing up we had winters

i saw snow so high

we could build a snowman and his house

we could snow ride and scream

while gliding down the white hills

it was so freezing cold our noses turned red and blue

our windows were frozen

our hearts longed for hot tea and warm meals

growing up we had springs

we saw all our trees growing into bright, light greens

we saw all our flowers blossoming

bees and insects coming to drink and celebrate

butterflies dancing in the fresh air

we smelled the beginning of a new season

the season of growing and blooming

of changing our wardrobes

and saying goodbye to our coats

at least for the next season

growing up we had summers

summers in which we walked barefoot

and ate from the bushes berries, cherries, plums

with worms in them

we threw them back to the bushes laughing

and looked around what to eat and try out next

hopefully the bees, insects and worms left

some of the fruits untouched - it was a feast

a little swimming pool and trying to build our own

lakes and rivers by using only a spoon

smelling the freshly cut grass

was one of my favorites

cooking outdoors and bringing some toys

to play in the grass

hearing the sound of summer

it was a blast

growing up we had falls

it was still warm sometimes fresh

everything turned red and yellow

sometimes we felt mellow

and wondered about change

we took our bicycles and rode through the rain

we saw seas

of deep red leaves

lying on the ground

making some sound

the wind asked them for a dance

they danced for us and the birds and the squirrels

to let them know

hurry to fly away and move on

hurry to collect the hazelnuts and walnuts

to bury them deep in the ground

still soft and wet

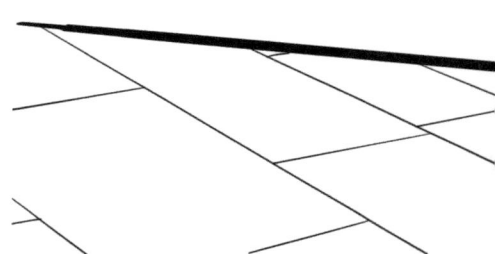

they could survive the next winter
and if we were lucky
we would witness a little walnut tree
when we waited long enough
through the upcoming seasons

cycle of seasons

i once loved a man

who couldn't love himself

i thought if i could pour down on him

the love that i had for him

i thought if i could show him

what i saw in him

that i could fix him

i once expected a woman to be

a woman that respected me with tenderness

how could i expect something from her

that she couldn't even be for herself

i thought if i told her

i forgive you

that she could forgive herself

i thought if i showed her what love meant

she could love her and me

i once thought i could fix and heal

by living as an example

by giving my energy and praying for healing

i thought i could turn them into beings

who are healed and free

and therefore able to love me

that's not the case

it's an endless job i took on

a job that wasn't even mine to begin with

the only one i could fix

is me

it also means that i am free

the only responsibility i have

is the one to me

responsibility

am i a feminist?

i am for equality

if standing for equal rights between all of humankind

means being a feminist

i am

i am an equalitist

if you moved on

but the people around you

are still willing to drown

in sorrow and bitterness

in yesterday and jealousness

it's because you took responsibility for where you are

it's because you listened to your gut

your instinct

your intuition

now you need to forgive them

now you need to allow yourself to move on

to love them from a distance

don't feel guilty for your growth

sometimes people fuel themselves with energy

when surrounded by others

some people give their energy

when surrounded with others

they are not necessarily at peace when they are alone

what they need to learn

is that they need to choose wisely

with whom to share their energy

because givers sometimes attract takers energy

when they meet with other givers

suddenly they will turn into extroverts too

suddenly they will fuel themselves with energy

it's called exchange

it's called choosing wisely

find your tribe

there is something we are

more scared of than believing in mystical powers

more scared of forgiveness

more scared of sickness

it's change

in fact

we are so scared of change

that we declare everything that would cause us to change

boohoo

continue denying

everything is changing

when you have something to say

say it

but remember

when you have nothing to say

that brings value

that shares your truth

that brings good

that is kind

that uplifts

that inspires

that is seeking to understand

don't

know when to shut up

sharing a meal with someone

is like an invitation to closeness

it's giving your time

your taste

your money

your skills

your energy

opening the doors to your home

and then offering what you made

spending time together

sharing your thoughts, ideas, empathy and laughter

there's something so beautiful and vulnerable in that

never turn down an invitation if you can

they are offering a lot more than simply some food

closeness

when i start to think

doubts come up

is what i write about too personal

is what i want to share too visible

too vulnerable ?

what will people say who know me?

what will the world think about me?

will they look at me and think silently

something not good about me?

what if they won't judge in silence?

will i drag people i love and care about into a mess?

how could i dare speak my truth

when they involve someone who is not me?

yes! it's so personal

yes! it's so visible

yes! it's so vulnerable

i will hope to be of help

i will hope that this is good

i am worried that hope won't catch me

i am brave enough to trust anyway

when i think

maybe you'll say
look there is a brave woman

maybe you'll say
wow - this is helping me

maybe you'll say
this is resonating with me

maybe you'll say
this is what i needed to hear

when i pray

when you hike in the woods

when you walk through the city

when you cook, clean or doing laundry

when you dance

when you sing

when you paint

when you create from your heart

when you look through the crowd

when you hold the intention

connect to your higher mind

i had issues with my father
i had issues with my mother
i had issues with strangers

i don't have daddy issues
i don't have mommy issues
i don't have social anxiety

there is a difference

it's a choice
whether to be aware
whether to choose fear
whether to heal

or not

how fascinating hair can be

something so simple that everybody has

growing out of our body

like nails

what humans make of it is so unfair

we use hair to spot race

we use hair to tell whether you're beautiful or not

we use long hair as a sign of femininity

we use short hair to spot masculinity

we use it to judge immediately

hair

telling someone

i can't do that for you

i'm sorry, that's not possible

i'm afraid i can't make it happen for you

unfortunately not

no

why is something so easy

so simple

so hard to say?

think of yourself as a business

any request that comes in

has to go through your rulebook

within your opening hours

respectfully

service-oriented

telling your customers what you can and cannot do

i hope for your understanding

but these are my conditions

book of rules

the hard part is not the knowing

what is right

what to do

how to be

it's doing it anyway

besides all the inconvenience

besides all the entertainment

besides all the bad feelings

besides the laziness

deep down

in our guts

we know exactly what's right

or wrong

i love giving hugs

when we both want to

when we need to have a big fat hug

when we need the feeling of love and protection

of closeness and warmth

of support and understanding

when it's safe to be so close to someone and just be

i don't like giving hugs

'cause you want me to

'cause you need assurance from me

'cause you need to feel we are okay

'cause you should say sorry but instead

you are going in for a hug

it's a trap

agenda

if you seek out to find the beliefs you bought into

limiting you to live up to the real you

simply ask yourself why i chose to believe in you

how come i still believe you are serving me any good?

the answer will be given to you

it has to reveal itself to you

if you find out that the belief is no longer benefiting you

if it's some bullshix that you picked up as a kid

you'll automatically drop it

and choose to believe in

what's more in alignment with you

i enjoy painting

when i forget about color theory

and only listen to my intuition

what feels right

which color is calling me

which subject matter is close to my heart

whatever speaks to me

when i do that

i enjoy painting

otherwise its work

having fun while floating in the unknown

i consume you

when i'm hungry for love

when i do something great

when i want to explore different cultures

when i'm sad

when i want to celebrate life

when i want to celebrate death

when i'm bored

when i'm sick

when i'm meeting friends

when i want to bring back memories

when i'm at a gathering

when i'm alone

when i want to procrastinate

when i'm stressed

when i want to build a new tradition at my house

i serve you

that's sad

'when i'm hungry' wasn't even on the list

food

an apple never falls far from the tree

i know i fell on the other side of the universe

stupid sayings

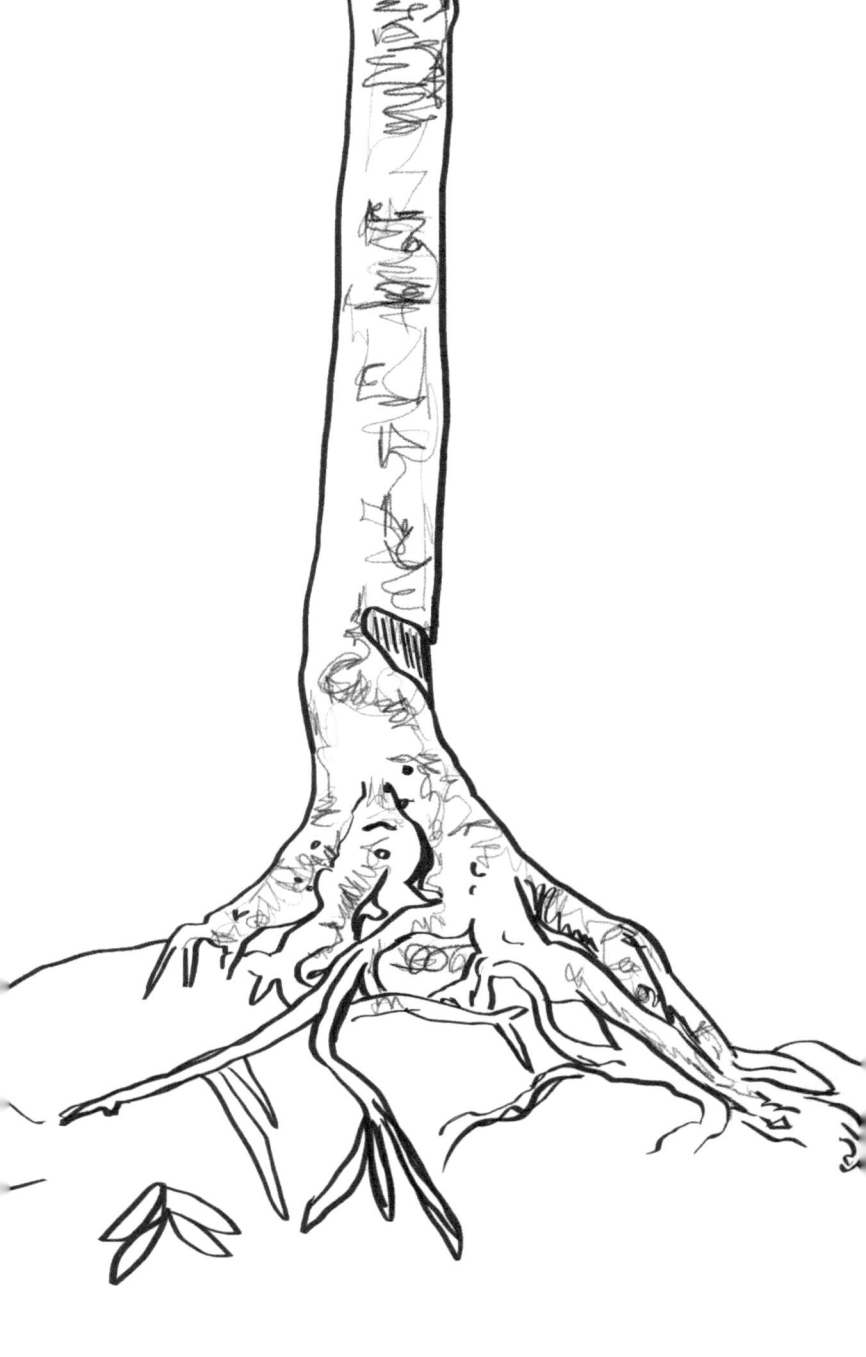

i'm not scared of being depressed

i think it's fine to be **depressed** from time to time

it's being sad, a little numb

it's feeling stuck, a little worried

it's figuring out how to solve this state of mind

to grow and come out of it

alone

when i'm on the other side

more wise

i'll share with you what made me so quiet

it's taking a deep rest from what you are currently being

it forces you to look inside of you

to find the ocean of light within you

and make up your mind

without the state of mind from outside of you

hoping for your understanding when i'm quiet

from time to time - i simply rediscover myself again

the sun is shining

the weather is easy

my mood is light

i find relaxation in the bright

the rain is pouring

the weather is breazy

my mood is wandering

i find relaxation in my mind

don't blame the weather

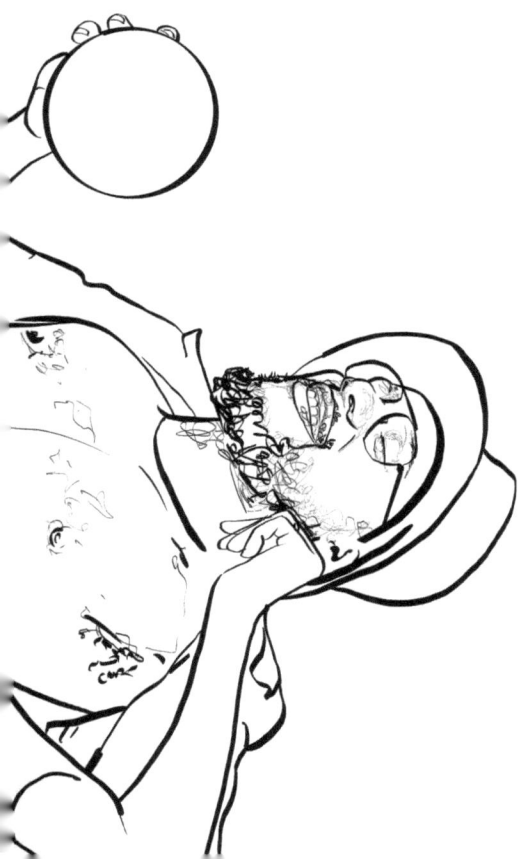

imagine

once you were living in white light

so bright

humans couldn't open their eyes

imagine

you lived under the wing of creator of life and love

and everything in between

imagine

once you chose to be born as a human being

to bring these lights and love amongst all beings

imagine

you even chose your own path and people you'll meet

and what seems to be your enemies

but you sat with them before

to make some agreements

to create your path, your experiences

played out in a world in which you were given

the gift of free will and duality

what a journey

imagine

when this shall be truly happening

it can only play out

by giving up all your memory

your soul would always live on in golden lights

to keep whispering to your human body and mind

and hope you'll get the message

and remember your true being

remember ?

when you are listening to this and thinking

i wonder is this my awakening?

if you are listening to this and thinking

could this be happening?

what this is bringing to you and your heart

is deconstructing what blind beings put into your feelings

so now

while truth hits

with goosebumps like angels blowing magic at you

you need to trust more in what your eyes can't grasp

you need to trust in your unseen ears

and listen to the whispers of your soul

still sitting in these golden lights

singing songs of guidance all through the night

it means trusting in magic and believing in wonders

to create healing and gift yourself meaning

it means spreading love to me and you is true

it's what you came here to do

remember

first you have to learn

how **you** work

before you can make the world work

you

if you can't feel

the stars
the music
the plants
the colors
the earth…

you can't create

imagination is your technology

when you strip down all your limiting beliefs
what will be left?

a spectrum of all there is

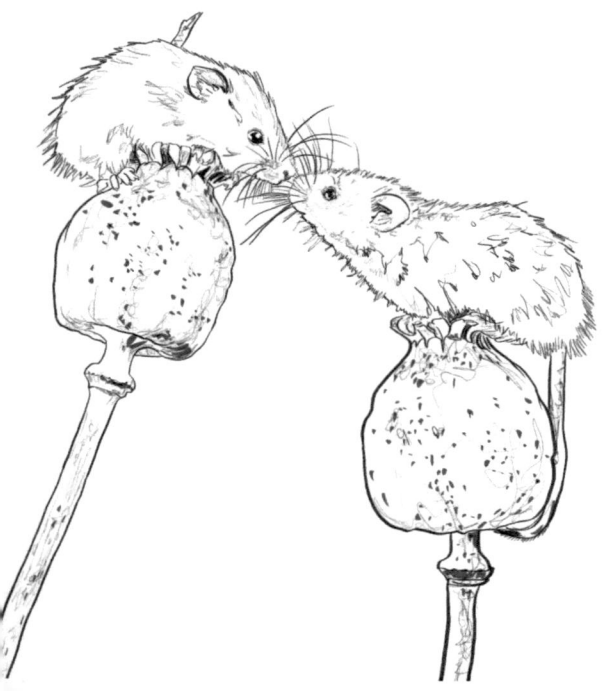

there is no one like **you**

there has never been anyone like **you**

the fact that you exist and reading this

is proof that we need **you** to be here right now

we need **you** to be **you** right now

be yourself

be authentic

know thyself

we need the most authentic version of you

it takes a village to raise a kid

why do we even think it's possible to raise a child alone

and not feel resentment?

not feel overwhelmed?

and not cause ourselves to break?

i am me, a mother

i'm not her dad, her sister or an uncle

i'm not the aunt, the neighbor or her grandmother

i'm not the bus driver who waits a little too long

to make sure she gets off the right stop

i'm not the eyes and ears

the hearts and tears

of a village

i am me, a mother

as are you
you are mothering too
because you are part of a village
part of a community
you are part of you and me
and therefore
i need you to be there for me and my kid

i need you to sit with her for a moment
see her, smile at her and acknowledge her
i need you to pick her up when she falls
and make a funny, silly face just for her
to remind her that the village is kind
the village is safe
and i'm proud to be a part of it

they say more people are dying of loneliness

than from cancer

loneliness is the number one disease

i'm inviting you to be a part of me

come and join me in raising my kids

i can't be thousands of people when i'm only me

i need you to join me

and share your presence for a second

to listen to her magic

not to tell yours

to give her time

not steal mine

to share a moment of light

instead of pointing out my darkness

to give me opportunities because i'm a mother
not because i am not

to give me hope because i am a mother
not because i am not

offer a smile, offer some love
offer me money, maybe a job
because i am a mother

i need support, not just from one, not just one time
i am asking you to be there all the time
i am asking for help in this lifetime

i am asking you
hundreds of you, thousands and millions of you
we need you

we are family

we are one

so act like one

you, the man, the woman, the teen and the child

we need you all

you are the brother i need

the man i don't have

the grandparents i so desire

the patience i long for

the cook, the lover

the mother i need to be able to mother

can you please be there for me?

can you take care with me?

can you be my family?

my village?

my tree?

sincerely,

all single mothers on earth

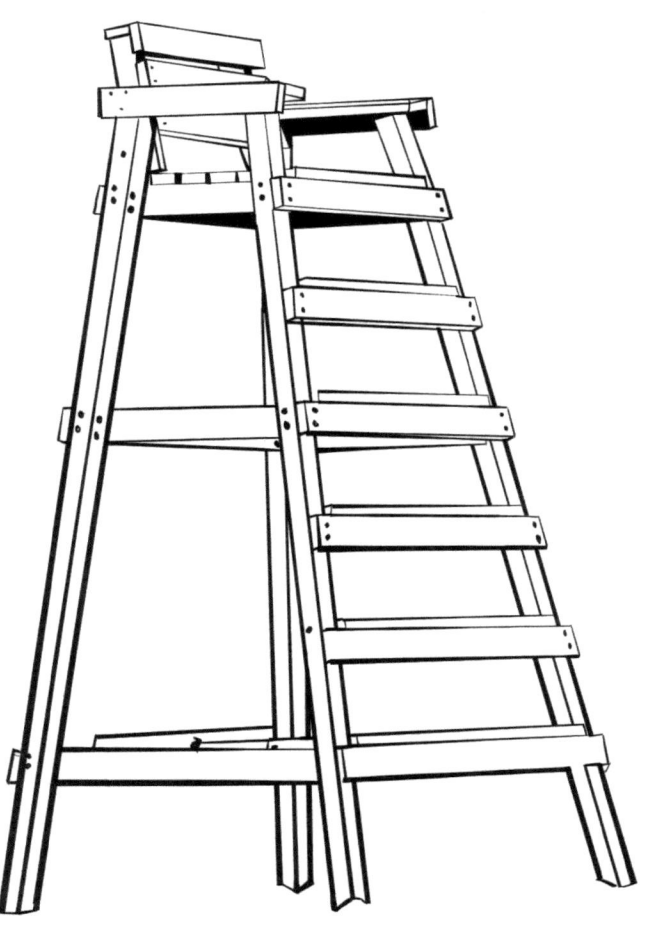

i would love to have a pick up service

to a horse ride club or an animal shelter once a week

i want the pick up service

to be like a community truck full of love

like a mini-fun-van

that's what i want, every week, at least once

i want to know that the horses, dogs, cats and cows

chooses the children and vice versa

that they have time to cuddle

to care, to have fun, to lay in the sun

to be without doing, to enjoy without performing

to feel without pressure, to learn what **they** desire

and when they need to say goodbye, see you soon

the fun van comes by to pick them up and drop them off

but more than that, to offer them love

is that too much to ask for?

should i put this on my vision board?

is it even possible to know they are taking care of?

they have been exposed to love outside of me?

that's what i want to see: a day each week offered for free

i would love to have an animal nature fun day

full of love and beingness

just one day of the week for my kids

to take the pressure off

if you do that for her

i will have enough energy to nurture me

if you do that for her

i will have enough on this earth

to open my arms and welcome her in my worth

if you do that for her

i will have prepared her bed to snuggle and cuddle

and read her favorite fairytales

to open the windows and greet the stars with her

and welcome the night

share hopes and dreams and say

good night, darling

see what's out there, darling

look at your heart, darling

what are the songs of your heart?

what are the joys and tears?

what are the laughs and fears of your heart, darling?

i will be able to listen

because i had time to listen to myself before

because you stepped in before

thank you for helping to raise a new generation with me

a generation that has felt what it means

to step in for each other's needs

wow!

what will come out of that?

what do you believe will happen if we do that?

fun truck

to give

is a gift for you

to shine

is the essence of you

to cry

is to release what no longer belongs to you

to live

is to mirror you

to praise

is the act of gratitude

how our children help us to see

how this book came to me

one day my daughter asked me

what i really want to do in life

a question that was haunting me in silence

all the time

suddenly the question appeared out loud

from a person's mouth i love and value

from a soul that teaches me light and virtues

i knew what i was about to answer

was the truth i couldn't bear to look at

to reveal to myself yet

i opened my mouth and shame appeared

and my mind went all weird

what my heart knew to be true

my mind questioned

it felt like a war zone

between knowing and fear

between desire and shame

between dreaming and the habit of staying

between certainty and **am i worthy?**

i knew right then and there
i was able to lie to myself
but i couldn't dare lie to her
i couldn't tell my girl to dream big
and not even admit my own dreams
it made me sick

so i told her
i want to write a book
i know i should write a book
i had several mystical experiences
like this one time
in the middle of the night...

stepping into your truth

selfless?

how is it a good thing

if yourself is less?

how is it even possible?

it's just wrong

'cause yourself can never be less

when we are one

it's save to be seen now

to show my light now

to invite myself to see the world now

self

i am a healer

it means that

i demand the light

to shine through

like a lamp

like you

are you aware of the language

your higher mind is using

to be able to speak to you?

excitement

whatever you believe in will come true
because that's the energy you hold on to

we know that to be true collectively now

what is not quite so clear to the collective is
how to examine what we believe to be true
and that we can instantaneously and easily
change what we believe
to beliefs we prefer more by now
and that all beliefs we hold on to
make us believe
they serve us in some way
and therefore are beneficial to us every day
i bet you didn't know that
yes, even those beliefs keeping us from what we so desire

usually it's fear of death, aloneness or worthiness

of something we bought into to feel safe

that's ridiculous and yet we are living it

whenever you feel

you cannot act on what excites you right now

be still for a moment and ask yourself why

right now

what do i believe to be true that makes me think

i can't act on this right now?

what will happen when my dream were real?

what is the worst thing that will happen if i pursue this?

dig, dig deep

examine yourself

visualize what you believe would happen

let it be shown to you

use your imagination if you must

i promise you the answer is not going to hurt you

even if it makes a fuss

even if the belief fears to be set aside

it thinks it's about to die

it will make you look the other way

in order to live in you further and stay

so reassure your belief that you are thankful

that it kept you 'safe'

that it will not die, it can exist

but please be quiet right now

because you're allowed to see

and view the other option

you always have the option to choose what you buy into

you are the creator

examine what you create from

the energies you are holding onto

align your beliefs with your liking

it's instantaneous

it's exciting

right now

staying warm

you

the driver take advantage of this device

called gps system

it's designed to tell you how

it will work for you and tell you the second

you on your **move**

so you can relax and don't need to worry about the how

you don't worry because you trust

that everyone is doing it's job

everyone is doing what they are suppose to do

so you can relax and even listen to music and sing a song

during moving to the unknown

oh, you say you know all this already?

imagine you pressure your car mentally so hard

expecting it to know

where it should go

when its only job is to use its engine and start moving

you

the driver knows where to go

that's something your car will never know

even if you pressure it, it can't succeed in it

you

the driver sometimes

especially when your dream destination seems far away

when your dream destination isn't your usual way

if you spontaneously wanna visit places unknown to you

when you fear to get lost

then please explain to me
how come you're still not on the move?

why do you keep postponing asking yourself
what's my dream destination?

and why is it then that you take your car as an excuse
because it doesn't know how to get there ?

so smooth of your limiting beliefs

it's hilarious that your belief is managing hiding so well
and make a fool out of you
just to rule over an old version of you

let your higher self do it's job and navigate you
it simply has the better view

if you are still reading these lines

and are maybe even hungry for more

do you know what this means?

it means that it resonates with you

it means there's hope for me and you

to wake up collectively

and shift into a new earth energy

actually it means we have already shifted

change will reveal itself

it's momentum

the outside is about to reflect it soon

don't be fooled

you have already shifted

it just seems like you haven't

it's like the trick they use in movies called continuity

but even though everything around you might look the same

you have changed already

don't feel discouraged

just act accordingly

to your new energy

and trust in all the new possibilities

we are shifting to a new realities all the time

let's say

a billionaire would like to test some theories of this book

let's say only one would be enough to

let's say, provide a whole country the freedom

to safely explore their excitements for one year

without wondering how to provide for themselves

without the fear of food and shelter

let's say all the basic needs of each person

will be provided for

imagine a whole country not needing

to work as we know it

let's say each and everyone can wake up in the morning

and think, what do i wanna do now?

and now? and now?

each moment simply follow

what their excitement is telling them to do

as it is written here in this book

simply following their excitement

as guided by their higher minds

when excitement are guidelines from our higher minds
this should work for a whole community
a whole country, the whole world
we would be guided and trust in synchronicities
that my highest excitement is of incredible value for all
that each and every single one is beneficial
to the overall

that those who wanna heal and examine their beliefs
meet the ones that work with energy
those who enjoy gardening will grow the food
those who enjoy cleaning will take care of this service
those who love to teach will be teaching
out of the love they carry
those who love to lead will provide that need
those who love going for walks will connect nature & talks
those who love to organize will help others to thrive
those who like to wonder around and count the clouds
can simply be appreciated for that

remember not to judge and trust in the process

there is no such thing as being lazy

sometimes we need to observe, wonder and be still

there's a need for that

it's all happening in cycles

everything changes

putting pressure on something that's not working

never helped

we are allowed to just be

just be sad

just be funny

just tell stories

just talking to strangers

when did we start valuing some actions more than others

who started with that?

and do we have to continue doing that?

why do we pay actors millions while telling children to
stop acting out their fantasies and fit in
fit into what?

by questioning what we've always done and saying
let's say and what if
what would it take to test this new understanding
we would do what albert einstein and all great minds did
questioning if there are better ways
it started with questioning and let's say
and let's allow
let's explore
let's see
let's play

let's say it wouldn't even take a billionaire

not even a millionaire

not even a government

let's say

it started with you

if you close your eyes and imagine

you are being kissed or making love

your body reacts and becomes aroused

because it doesn't know the difference

between imagination and your physical reality

if you close your eyes and imagine a funny scene

your body will react and start smiling

maybe even laughing

you'll feel joy and forget about your current reality

if you think about who you wish to become

if you connect to a parallel reality one

explore how she thinks and acts

let yourself feel this other reality

explore what she does all day differently

you can unlock the same potential

you can actually feel

the difference in vibration

you can feel how she feels

the possibility of using imagination as a technique

every genius we witnessed on earth so far

was a dreamer before

being called a liar

a threat to man in power

to governments and religious leaders

who used the power of planting fear in people

to create a society which strengthens their power

every genius risked their reputation

and used their imagination

every genius planted the seed of trust instead

and consumed the images of imagination further ahead

every genius was driven by creation

not by money

not by fame

certainly not by being liked

by those who fear creation

every genius protected their technique

to stay safe and alive

so no one could plant fear and doubt

on their way to the sky

every genius couldn't care less if they failed

their definition of failure was different from ours

theirs was redirecting and aligning again

they couldn't tell their secret out loud
they would have been so proud

because true geniuses share their knowledge out loud
as long as they are not facing being hanged or bound

but they love to share ideas and concepts
they love to question the known
and believe more in the songs of the unborn

you can think of them as transitioners
first contacters

now is a different time

we remember again collectively

we are safe to speak and explore unexpectedly

we are capable to quantum jump now

and risking being called stupid and foolish now

we won't die

we won't be silenced

maybe we would be called stupid, foolish

maybe dump or a dreamer

maybe lazy or a failure

so what

it's the risk you take and the legacy of the path of a genius

i would say

if it works for you, you have won

if it has value for the whole society

than you are called a genius

otherwise you simply risk being a happy fool

the important part here

to be clear

is not being driven by fear

creation

don't hope for the best

don't hope to be of use

don't hope for it to work out

don't try to grow

don't try to make it work

don't try to do your best

unless you want to try and hope forever

because trying and hoping are states in themselves

either

i'm trying to do the best that i can

or

i'm doing the best that i can

either

i'm hoping everything will turn out in my favor

or

i know everything will turn out in my favor

can you feel the difference in energy

that each statement holds?

nature doesn't need us to survive

nor stones

nor minerals

nor crystals

nor water

nor air

nor the sun

nor the moon

nature crafted mother earth so that we can survive

it's us humans who need them to thrive

we need them to survive

but instead we feel superior

we were given free will and a faded memory

so we can go on this journey called life

a school to remember our true selves

isn't that fun?

isn't that exciting?

you are what you think
because thinking is a thing
your thoughts come before you speak
before you seek, before you make
look around you

it's all made by you

i am waiting for permission from the world to see me
before i take the mic and step on stage

i am waiting for a thousand things to come into my life
before i gift myself permission to shine

if this is you as well
if this sounds familiar as hell
know that what we are waiting for
is ourselves

take your power back

a bunch of magnets spend all their time

trying to figure out how to magnetize

how to attract

you don't need to learn how to magnetize baby

you are a magnet baby

look around you and see what you've already magnetized

you are a powerful magnet already

do you want to magnetize more self worth

money, abundance, joy and gratitude

friendships, soul connections and love?

then change your inner frequency

get rid of old definitions

and fill your magnetic container with love energy

that's all there is to it

is that too easy for you?

then ask yourself why do you hold on to the belief

that life has to be hard and complicated baby

magnet

i am light

i am dust

i am a soul

having a human experience

stones hanging from the ceiling

light enters, turning every corner, every hole

into spectrums of light

when sunshine hits a crystal, it becomes color

and you enter the spectrum of all possibilities

become a crystal

crystal clear

so light can shine through you

shine all spectrums of love

color, abilities and healing through you

become a crystal

fearless, unbiased, egoless, opinionless

become clear to reflect light

and bring colors through

you might meet the sun at night

and rainbows in the sea

it all could happen

once you are free

rainbow room

do you know

when you know that you have truly changed?

when your outside circumstances haven't changed

but your response is

your reaction is

your actions are

you thoughts are

then your life has no choice but to rearrange

remember?

life is your mirror

reflecting your change

most people wait for their reflection to shift

before they change their own ways or lift

see the problem here?

the solution starts with where you stand

i'm so sick and tired of playing small

holding on to fear and shame's cruel call

tired of hiding from my true self's light

fearing overprotection and running from my might

what's the worst thing that could happen?

i may die?

when i know for sure

once i exist

i know i always fly

existence can't be destroyed

it only transforms

so what's the worst thing that could happen?

i end up alone?

when i know for sure, no-one is ever alone

what's the best thing that could happen?

let's ask that too!

i could claim who i am

and shift to a reality where that's true

i am a freaking awesome healer

a powerful channel

i can bring immense value to my community

and inspire those tuned into my frequency

i am a transformative artist

who brings codes to people's homes through my artistry

changing their hearts

and their spaces to higher frequencies

i am a writer

i hear whispers and turn them into words

sending them out energetically through poetry

through stories

i am publishing what came through me

and will transform a whole society

i freaking claim that i am

i live that

i will act before the doors open

and thank the universe that the doors will open

i am acting on my intuition and on my heart's desires

this is proof of it

i am living proof of it

so, who do you claim to be?

who do you know yourself to be

but are still scared of admitting to yourself ?

i want you to please claim it

and share it

and act on it

and trust in yourself

trust that the doors will open once you start walking

i want you to share that with the world

and tag me

so i can help you announce it to the world

that you have found your worth

and enable us to reflect your worth back to you

i am so proud of you

i love you

being sick of it is your sign

it's your turn now

there's nothing worse
than not living an authentic life

there's nothing more soul-crushing
than doing what's not in alignment with your purpose

there's nothing that saddens your heart more
than denying your soul's calling

there's nothing that makes your body temple sicker
than restricting the values you bring

there's simply nothing more important
than living your life's purpose

there's nothing more vital
than aligning your joy with the joy of your soul

there's nothing that brings more abundance
than the value you offer by being your truest self

there's nothing that brings you more joy
than igniting the light in your brother's eye

there's nothing healthier for your body and mind
than the peace you radiate in your sister's mind
by welcoming peace into your life
through aligning your heart with your higher mind

there's simply nothing more important
than living the meaning of your life
and bringing value to each other's lives

bliss

yesterday

is the memory

of someone

who you used to be

tomorrow

is the memory

of someone

who you choose to be

goodbye

see you soon

we are connected

always

like drops of water

that build the ocean

creating life itself

trough transformation in different cells

in different forms

maybe we'll become drops of rain

or tears in someone's eye

maybe a snowflake in the winter sky

goodbye

see you soon

in a different way

my next book is on it's way

to all the photographers
who inspired the illustrations in this book
my deepest gratitude goes out to you

to my daughter and her beautiful friends, thank you for
sharing these moments with us and allowing me to transform
your beautiful experiences into illustrations
you have brought love and life into these illustrations

photo credits
roya emilia pommer, mali lua woodall, carla sauer,
anna schuster, matteo sauer

to unsplash.com and all the talented photographers from around the world who share their artistry, i celebrate you! for the majority of images used, i have credited the respective photographer's
for a few images where the photographer's
name could not be determine, i extend my gratitude to unsplash.com

photo credits: unsplash.com
john moses bauan, vlad sargu, christina gottardi,
kristen sturdivant, craig philbrick, pablo rebolledo,
annie spratt, yannis h, toa heftiba, paul wong,
húng nguyen viet, alex knight,torn lee, jacek dylag,
ryoji iwata, peng cheng, benjamin voros, ben moreland,
vincent van zaling, nick fewings, brian mc mahon,
whereslugo, julian myles, yanapi senaud, engin akyurt,
maurits bausenhart, mike van den bos, sunguk kim, janosch
diggelmann, eileen kummer, gilles rolland-monnet,
chris briggs & more

breathe

retrospective

about the author

mitra is an artist, a healer, and an author
as a channel and energy healer, she deeply believes in the
transformative power of energy and creativity for healing
her work is designed to help individuals connect with their inner
selves and harness their own healing potential
through her art and energy healing sessions, she offers guidance
and support for personal growth and spiritual awakening

if you feel drawn to her art, you can find more in mitra's shop
where she offers a variety of unique artworks
including paintings and prints
she also provides energy healing sessions and spiritual guidance to
explore her offerings and connect with her
visit her online shop **mitraart.com** and follow her on social media
find mitra on instagram, tiktok, and facebook **@mitraart0**

shop

instagram

about this book

loud is not just a collection of poetry and art

it's a divine creation

channeled from mitra in just a few days

it embodies three years of deep personal growth and healing

as mitra embraced self-worth, self-love, and freed herself from

toxic influences

stepping into her true power

featuring **99 illustrations** created by mitra

including scenes with her children and their friends

the book offers a visual feast that complements its spiritual

message

this collection of poetry and art reflects a transformative

journey and aims to inspire and awaken readers to their own

authentic selves

reading this book is not just an experience

it's a chance for a profound shift towards your true self

prepare for a transformative journey that will deeply impact

your life